T0374014

Poems from a Higher Place

JESUSHESUS

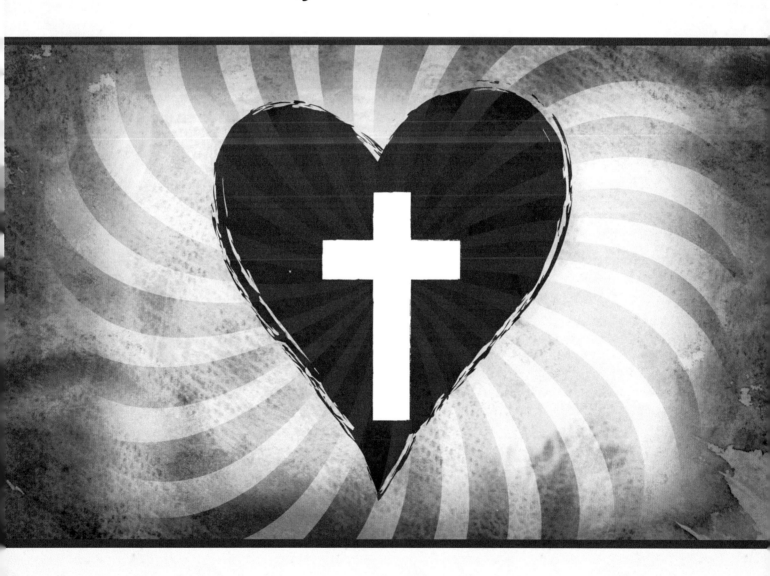

Donna M. Heinzen

WestBow Press books may be ordered through booksellers or by contacting:

WestBow Press
A Division of Thomas Nelson & Zondervan
1663 Liberty Drive
Bloomington, IN 47403
www.westbowpress.com
1 (866) 928-1240

ISBN: 978-1-4908-7762-4 (sc)
ISBN: 978-1-4908-7758-7 (e)

Library of Congress Control Number: 2015906669

Print information available on the last page.

WestBow Press rev. date: 05/11/2015

WESTBOW
PRESS
A DIVISION OF THOMAS NELSON
& ZONDERVAN

Contents

Love

Have you ever wondered why

We try to destroy our own lives by our actions?

Through the power of our tongues, we control the outcome of our situations

It's time to start whispering people it's time to tame the beast within

Let us stop hurting others by continuing to be who we've been

Nothing good ever came out of harsh words and resentment

It's time to put our hands together and rise up from discontentment

Take pride in our Lord Jesus Christ, and the fact that He

Only needed to speak softly to part the Red Sea

His words were filled with love so that we might see that

Togetherness, not apart is where we should be

So say to your neighbor, your brother, your friend, "I'm

Sorry, I love you, and this is the end",

There'll be no more quarreling, for the past is the past

And start building a future that was meant to last

One with love and peace and compassion

Tired of your wardrobe? Start wearing these and you'll be in fashion

For the whole world stands to gain from this small task

Just love your neighbor as yourself

This is all I ask

Positive

Remember the sign, the positive sign

When things aren't looking so good or going your way,
don't look towards the negative, don't go astray

Stay focused on the sign, the positive sign, for we
know this is the truth, the light, the way

The way to peace, joy and salvation, not negativity, hatred and condemnation

These are all negatives that come from Satan, for he
wants us to be broke and not full of salvation

Nothing good ever came from the negative. Keep your
eyes steady and focused on the positive

For we are nothing if we have equal amounts of both so
offset this equation and keep adding the word

So all that He promised will be heard

Stand up and shout it from here to there. Start increasing
the positive so our harvest we may share

And feast on the blessings He so freely gives to us who believe that He truly lives

Focus on the positive, that which is the cross +

Remember not the negative or the things of the past

For we have gained so much more that is meant to last

For He was, is and always shall be the most we could ever hope for

Positively

Amen

Take a Moment

Sing praises to our Father, our Almighty King

For He is ruler over all and Master of Everything

He is the creator of all we see and hear and touch

He gave this world, this life, this day to us because He loves us so very much

So take each moment and soak it in

The glory of God our Father and feel His spirit within

Look around in amazement at all you see and hear

And know that God's handy work created it all and He is near

So take a moment and sing praises to the King

For He gave us life, He gave us everything

Thank you Father for all you have done

But most of all, thank you for your Son

It is through Him, we are saved

That is the greatest gift you ever gave

Thank you, Thank you, Thank you, Lord

We praise your holy name

We ask all those who believe

To take a moment and do the same

The Voice Within

The voice within is always there

Should we listen? Do we dare?

For what if it tells us things we do not wish to hear?

The voice within is telling us that Jesus is near

He guides us all the way

He walks each step with us each and everyday

He cares, He loves, He is our Father, just because

He rights us when we're wrong and when we are weak, He is strong

He lives in us so others may see His love and honesty

Don't be afraid of the voice within for that which guides us through thick and thin

But know and follow what He says each time

So our hearts will grow in love and get rid of the grime

That causes our people to be thoughtless and blind

To say things and do things without a conscious mind

Remember He is here with us and keep His words close

For in Him we live and gain the most

Be all that we can be through Christ our Sovereign Lord

For what have we got to lose

How much more can we afford?

Keep Pressing On

When your heart aches so much and nothing seems

To turn out right no matter what you do

You keep climbing up that hill, but the ground keeps slipping under your feet

You want to be going somewhere, anywhere, but anger

And disappointment are all you meet

You want to hang on to something, but nothing seems to last

Grab a hold of my love and let go of the past

Reach for the Truth, the Light, the Son

Keep plugging through, Keep Pressing on

Make your way through the storm and the rain

Let go of the hurt, let go of the pain

Reach for the Truth, the Light, the Son

Keep plugging through, Keep pressing on

Keep pressing on in the word, your faith and belief

Things will turn around and you will find relief

Just keep pressing on with God's plan for you

And you will see a difference in everything you do

For you are perfect in His eyes and that is the key

For He is the only one you need to be concerned with making happy

Life will always have it's ups and downs

Just keep plugging through

Keep pressing on

What Greater Love is This?

What greater love is this

Than the love of God our Father?

Who gave up His only Son

That us sinners may be saved

He who cared so much about

The well being of others

That he gave his Son

So we all could become brothers

Brothers in Christ to make up His church

To save us from sin, despair and defeat

To cleanse our spirit

So one day we will meet

Our loving Father in paradise, in splendor

That one day we will know and understand

The love of God our Father, so tender

For what greater love is this?

Different Now

I'm different now, I'm not the same

Some call me odd, some call me lame

I'm not the person I used to be

Or yet the one I want to become

I'm a work in progress can't you see

For your work is not done

I'll keep working each day

To follow your word in every way

To be the person you intended

From the beginning until this life has ended

Then I can say I have finished the race

When I climb up to paradise and see you face to face

I'll gasp at the awesomeness of what I will behold

When I see everything you promised

Everything I was told

For now, people can call me what they may

For it matters not what they say

For if I have you

Nothing else matters

At the end of the day

The Butterfly

The winds of change are blowing as you breathe new life in me

I feel your presence Lord, I feel the change within

There's a stirring of emotions, most of which are in my head

But strangely enough they are all calmed when I focus on you instead

A new "me" emerges each and everytime I am cleansed by your word

And I renew my mind

Transform me, change me and make me anew

Show me my destiny, my new life I live for you

Blow the winds of change in ever so strong

And make everything right that used to be wrong

My sins are forgiven, Praise the Lord!

So let me start over for I am reborn

That shameful page from the book of sin has been torn

I emerge from the dust basked in your glory and light

Behold, Jesus is in me and I've joined His fight

To keep Christians united and praising His name

Until He comes back and nothing will ever be the same

Glory be to God!

4 You

Take a look around

At everything He has created

The trees, the flowers, the birds

The sun, the moon and stars

It goes on and on

He created all this to be ours

To share with us all the beauty He has within

For us to appreciate all the good in this life

And to free us from sin

By the touch of His finger

All this beauty He did form

So that we may be reminded

That there is peace amidst the storm

Stop and take in the beauty, the sight, the sound

the taste, the smell

And know that because He lives in us

All is good and peaceful and well

Thank you, Jesus

Appreciation

Thank you Jesus for everything you do and everything you say

Thank you for the memories of yesterday,

The hope for tomorrow and the faith of today

Thank you for putting up with me when no-one else wants to

For loving me for the person I am on the inside

Which most of us forget to do

Thank you for making me different, wierd, unique

Thank you for your word which I diligently seek

Thank you for all the good things in my life

Thank you for my family, my husband, my wife

Thank you for the special moments I treasure

That are mine and yours alone

Thank you most of all Jesus, for being who you are

For creating me to love you and someday be beside you

As you are seated on your throne

The Truth

Once I was a sinner full of darkness and despair

I asked you into my life I needed someone to listen, someone to care

I gave my life to you Lord to save me from myself

To ask for forgiveness and to put my sins upon a shelf

A shelf you did not need for you wiped my sins clean away

Thank you, Thank you, Thank you Lord

Is all that I can say

Take Me To The River

Take me to the river

Where the water flows clear and fast

Wash me in your spirit, Lord

Fill me up and make it last

Cleanse me of my sins

Wash me of my iniquities

Free my soul from the chains it bears

Renew my mind from the sin that it wears

Take me to the river

Where life and love flow free

Take the blinders off

So that I can once again see

Take me to the river, Lord

And let your love flow through me

Stop Hurting

Who do you think you are trying to reopen that scar

Digging and scratching at that hurt within

I thought it was gone, I wish it had never been

Do you really know me? Do you see the hurt inside?

Why do you keep aggrevating, instead of helping it to subside?

We all need to be more careful with our words

Let's use them for love instead of as swords

For they can cut deep into wounds we are unaware

That people have, but are unwilling or too embarrassed to share

I know Lord, we are not supposed to take offense

But wouldn't it be easier using love as our defense?

If we thought before acting and did so with love

We would hurt fewer people and start healing

With your help from above

Give It Up

Give me your burden, give me your care

I will take it, I am always there

You don't have to go it alone

For cares are only yours should you want them to own

Let your yoke be light, your heart be free

Unstrap your burdens, give them to me

Walk through this life as carefree as a child

Knowing I am there to make each episode mild

Yes, there may be times when you stumble and fall

But you can overcome if you give me your burdens and give me them all

So let your heart be not troubled or your soul be in fear

But have the comfort of knowing that I am always here

Let your yoke be light, your heart be free

Unstrap your burdens, give them to me

Don't Stray

Something's not right today I can feel it within

I'm feeling a little "off" could it possibly be sin?

I forgot to praise you or put you first

Now I realize, it's a word from you that I thirst

Thank you for being the forgiving God that you are

For kindly reminding me not to wander off too far

If it wasn't for that feeling, I might never know

That seeking you is where I need to go

To fill that void, that empty space inside my heart

To ask for forgiveness and make a fresh start

Tomorrow will be better and today is looking up

Because I came to you and you filled my cup

Now if I could just remember day to day

That in your word is where I need to stay

My heart would never ache or feel this way

Please kindly remind me if I stray

Please keep me in line, this I pray

Thank you, Jesus

I'm A Winner

Capture the thoughts inside my head that hurt and torment me

And make me wish I were dead

Shake me and wake me and make me see

That it's only the devil trying to eat at me

He wants to kill, steal and destroy

So deep in my soul is where he desires to toy

To bring me down, deep into his pit

Into sadness and depression is where he wants me to sit

Now wait just a minute, knock that off!

You know the devils' tactics so at him you can scoff

Turn your thoughts around and change your day

Tell the devil to go to hell and that's where he can stay

Then stand up and shout, "Glory, Halleluiah, Hooray!"

For I won another battle with the devil today

Meeting Jesus, My Friend

Since I met you I'll never be the same

My thoughts and actions used to all be in vain

My life now has purpose, reason and rhyme

You saved me from myself just in the nick of time

You've opened my eyes to things I've never seen before

And showed me where I went wrong and what I need to do to restore

You welcome me with open arms each and every day

You never get angry or turn me away

I reach for you and you are always there

My deepest, darkest thoughts I can trust in you to share

You always give me guidance in your loving way

In your gentle arms is where I want to stay

Guide me, teach me, show me the way to find peace in you each and every day

To make the most out of every day, to live each moment as if it were my last

To hope for tomorrow and put yesterday in the past

To have a vision, a goal, a dream to produce a harvest for your team

So others may learn of your love and your glory

So we may continue to keep telling your story

Sharing salvation, peace and grace, spreading your word all over the place

'Till every knee will bow to praise your name

And all of creation shall never be the same

The Change

I used to go to church I guess for the sake to say

I made myself feel better because I took the time to pray

Once a week on a Sunday, about a half hour long

I'd feel so spiritual as I prayed and I knelt and I sang your song

Then I'd go back to my miserable life full of deceit and disgust and a whole lot of strife

I didn't give you a thought the rest of the week, for it wasn't Sunday, why of you should I speak?

I couldn't figure out why my life was so bleak. I finally hit rock bottom, the pit of

despair, I had nowhere to turn and I didn't even care

Until one day, the third of July, you sent a man into my life to open my eyes

He's a disciple of yours, I am sure. He told me of a new life, a treatment, a cure

He said to trust in you and everything would be okay. He kissed me then and my cares

went away

I married this man you sent into my life. He's my husband now and I am his wife

Together we're working as a well oiled machine waiting on miracles yet to be seen

We are learning and growing each step of the way

and loving each other more each and everyday

Thank you for this man you gave to me, the blessing you sent into my life

Help me to be a blessing to him and to be a good wife

To always put you first in everything we do

To praise you for longer than a half hour a week

For a good marriage, good life and your blessings we seek

Please help us reach our goal, our summit, our peak

And always remember that it's more of you we seek

My Helper From Above

There's an angel on my shoulder sent from God above

To watch over and protect me and surround me with His love

He watches over me each and everyday waiting for a chance to help me

Waiting for me to say

"I can't do this without you, can't you see?"

That's when my angel takes over and carries me

He digs me out of ditches, toils and snares

Through Jesus, he helps me, through Jesus, he cares

I might not even realize he is there

But I thank God that he is and thank God that he cares

Jesus Can

People can't change people so why do we even try

To continually change those that tend to make us cry

When will we realize that we shouldn't even try

To change people and just trust in Him and know

Jesus can, Jesus can

We tend to manipulate and fabricate to change the ones we love

We kick and scream and holler when push comes to shove

When really it's all so simple if we'd just remember Him from above

Jesus can, Jesus can

Quit trying so hard and just let go

Give it to Him in prayer and believe and know

That Jesus can, Jesus can

What If?

What if my days on earth were done?

And my race down here was run?

Did I make the most of everyday?

Did I share some laughter along the way?

Did I share the grace and love of Jesus with anyone?

Was I daring, did I have some fun?

Am I prepared for what lies ahead?

Life everlasting beyond the dead?

Did I prepare a way for the Lord?

Or did I just get tired?

Did I just get bored?

We only have one chance at this life, one race to run

Did I put forth the effort to do the most for our Son?

Will I be worthy when it's all said and done?

What if my days on earth were done?

Did I do enough for the Son?

Did I do enough for the freedom I won?

Think about it

Change!

I Care

Jesus help me! I can't take it anymore

Why did you create me? What am I living for?

I've made a mess of my life this I know

I have nothing productive, nothing to show

I blame everyone else 'cause it couldn't be me

Who's gotten myself into this mess and refuses to break free

Free of the addiction, free of the 'woe's me"

Free from the problems to which no end I see

Stop just a minute and start believing in me

I'm the ticket to your salvation, the means to set you free

Yesterday doesn't matter if you put your trust in me

Erase the chalkboard of all your past mistakes

Start over today and start living right for Heaven's Sake

I love you my son

It doesn't matter what you've done

Just put your faith in me

For I will set you free

Warning!

Listen people, can't you hear?

Time is running out, the end is drawing near

The signs of the times are telling us what the Bible said long ago

That times would get terrible and we would reap just what we sow

This world has gone crazy, atleast that's how it looks

The devil is running rampant and has dug his teeth in like hooks

To a society that cares more about outward appearances and looks

We need to start over, we need to do something right

We need to open our bibles and start living by the light

We need to start caring more about the appearance of our hearts

To heal them with God's word for that's where it all starts

For if we heal the hearts of men by the words of God our Father

This life would once again be worth living and not seem like such a bother

Let's spread God's word as far as we can, so we can live upright and worthy

And have respect for ourselves and others again

Time to Pray

Broken families, broken lives

Broken husbands, broken wives

Why can't we just see the place that we need to be

All this worry, all this sorrow

From yesterday right through to tomorrow

Does it have to be this hard?

Does it have to be this tough?

Was life meant to be like this?

Is it always going to be this rough?

It doesn't have to be, you know, if we would just remember where to go

In the shelter of the Most High is where we will find our rest

To recover from the darkness and merge forth to do our best

For only in our Savior can we find that inner peace

To find that solace within and make the demons cease

We must fight evil with good, that's what our Lord is saying

So let's stop fighting and let's start praying

Maybe we can regain some honor, respect and some pride

And be happier with one another once the demons subside

Remember a minute is only a minute

And a day is only a day

But what a difference a minute in a day makes

When we take the time to pray

Your Blessings Count

Count your blessings, one by one

Keep counting each and every one until the day is done

Always give thanks in every way and try to always have a kind word to say

To show each other we care in every possible way

For every person is a gift from God above

Given to us to treasure, given to us to love

And if we would remember to count our blessings, rather than counting our costs

We would see how much more we could gain and what little would be lost

If we are busy counting blessings, we have no time for curses

We would store many more treasures in Heaven

That are worth a million times more than we will ever have in our purses

Stop being superficial people and start being real

Stop caring about what people think

And start caring about how we all feel

Reflection

Take this simple test, it's as easy as one, two, three

Ask yourself this little question, am I who God intended me to be?

If so, "Way to Go!" If not, what have I forgot?

Am I carrying the fruits of the spirit? Do I have patience, peace, humility?

Or am I harboring turmoil, resentment and hostility?

Am I quick to forgive and to forget? Or do I hold on, remember and resent?

God intended us to be in the likeness of "He." So take a look at you, take a look at me

Reflection to reflection, is it Him that we see? Where is it, we need to be?

If we don't see God when we look at each other face to face

Maybe we need to study His word more and pick up the pace

For this day is almost over and a new one is set to begin

Are we going to continue to keep living in sin?

Time is of the essence. We need to start getting this right

Stop beating around the bush and start living by the light

Once we start doing this our lives become whole

Because we are able to take back everything that Satan stole

Our promises for tomorrow lie in our actions of today

So let's keep a watchful guard over the things we hear and see and say

To answer the question from the start, am I all that God intended me to be?

Comes from a loving attitude and a forgiving heart

It's never too late to start over. To say, "I'm sorry, I was wrong"

Just give it to God and let it be

That's how we start being who He intended us to be

Walk With Me

Take my hand and walk with me, open my eyes so I may see

That nothing is impossible and your help is free

If I remember to ask you just to walk with me

When life's struggles are getting me down

And the smile I used to wear has turned to a frown

Gently tap me on the shoulder and remind me

To ask you just to walk with me

You are my listener, you are my guide, you are the Great Advisor if in you I confide

And listen to my spirit and what you are trying to say

To turn the bad to good and change the outcome of my day

Help me to seek your guidance along the way

So please take my hand and don't let go

I need you Lord everyday and I want you to know

You're the one I'm living for and you're the reason why

I can do all things in this life and get by

Because I look forward to my future with you, starting the day I die

So friends and family don't cry for me when I'm gone. In fact throw a party, sing a song

For I have left this place of misery and strife. To go to my new home and my perfect life

To be with Jesus, to be His wife

What greater place is there to be?

So please don't cry for me

Great God

As I wait here in the darkness

And focus on your love

Meditate on your greatness

And wait for your touch from above

A scripture comes to me in my heart

That I can do all things through you

Our God from above

Grant me Lord, your healing hands

So I may work through you

And behold your greatness in everything you do

Work through me so others may see

The awesome experience of knowing you personally

Help me each day to walk and trust in your way

To leave yesterday behind and concentrate on today

Thank you Lord for the gifts you have given us

For they are far too many to repay

Don't Walk With The Devil

Is the devil knocking on your door again?

Is he showing up pretending to be your friend?

Are you holding his hand instead of mine?

Walking down that street of "woes me" again?

You pass the corner of hurt and offense

Right downhill to regret and defense

You finally come to a dead end called despair

When you realize once again

"Oh yeah! Jesus is there!"

Run quick, as fast as you can!

Run to me and let go of the devils' hand

I will always take you willingly back into my arms

Where you are safe and free from any harm

I will comfort you with my words, my promises and my love

The more you search for me

The more the devil will flee

The better off you will be

The good in yourself you will start to see

For what you'll have inside of you is me

How much better off could you possible be?

So why take a walk with the devil?

Instead take a walk with me

Miracles Can Happen

Miracles can happen, they most certainly do

But it's not just up to Jesus. It's up to me and you

He has the power to make it happen, but He needs our faith to see it through

You see, the only way He can work is through me and through you

Together in faith, no limits apply

To the wondrous things that can happen and the harvest He can supply

So keep your hearts focused and your faith at it's peak

If it's miracles, harvests and blessings that you seek

Rely on Jesus always and forever

But also remember, He needs you to be part of the endeavor

He will not interfere if we do not ask Him to intercede

And then have the faith and belief that He will supply our need

Don't give up hope, don't lose sight. Together in faith we shall win this fight

He'll take care of you, He'll take care of me. From His glorious riches in Christ you see

Now Glory be to God our Father forever and ever. And let our faith falter never

And we shall see what our Father is capable of

With our help from faith and His help from above

So don't give up hope or lose that faith

For the Father always delivers whatsoever He saith!

Amen

Sincerely,

JesusHesus Ministries

About the Author

Donna began hearing from the Lord shortly after becoming born again in December of 2011. Jesus began giving her and her husband Eric instructions and guidance on how to live and act in certain situations. He started putting poems in her spirit. She began writing them down. She had never been a poet, although she always excelled in English and found it to be one of her favorite subjects. She believes with all her heart that through the Holy Spirit, Jesus speaks to her through these poems so that they may be shared with others. Many of these poems deal with personal situations going on in their lives at that time. Jesus spoke to her and told her to publish a book when she had thirty poems finished. She is following His instructions and His calling upon her life. She believes we all are given gifts from God and the gift of poetry is one of hers. She hopes all who read this will find their special gifts from God and use them to serve Him and others.